KU-350-180

MOJANG

MINECRAFT

EGMONT
We bring stories to life

First published in Great Britain 2018 by Egmont UK Limited
The Yellow Building, 1 Nicholas Road
London W11 4AN

Written by Stephanie Milton
Additional material by Marc Watson, Emily Richardson, Karim Wallden, Filip Thoms,
Jennifer Hammervald, Patrick Geuder, Max Herngren and Amanda Ström.
Designed by Paul Lang and Ian Pollard
Illustrations by Ryan Marsh and Sam Ross
Cover designed and illustrated by John Stuckey
Production by Stef Fischetti and Laura Grundy
Special thanks to Lydia Winters, Owen Jones, Junkboy, Martin Johansson, Marsh Davies and Jesper Oqvist.

© 2018 Mojang AB and Mojang Synergies AB. MINECRAFT is a trademark or registered trademark of Mojang Synergies AB.

All rights reserved.

MOJANG

ISBN 978 1 4052 9112 5

68151/003
Printed in EU

ONLINE SAFETY FOR YOUNGER FANS
Spending time online is great fun! Here are a few simple rules to help younger fans stay safe and keep the internet a great place to spend time:

- Never give out your real name – don't use it as your username.
- Never give out any of your personal details.
- Never tell anybody which school you go to or how old you are.
- Never tell anybody your password except a parent or a guardian.
- Be aware that you must be 13 or over to create an account on many sites.
Always check the site policy and ask a parent or guardian for permission before registering.
- Always tell a parent or guardian if something is worrying you.

Stay safe online. Any website addresses listed in this book are correct at the time of going to print. However, Egmont is not responsible for content hosted by third parties. Please be aware that online content can be subject to change and websites can contain content that is unsuitable for children. We advise that all children are supervised when using the internet.

Egmont takes its responsibilty to the planet and its inhabitants very seriously.
We aim to use papers from well-managed forests run by responsible suppliers.

MOJANG

MINECRAFT

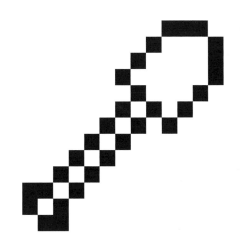

ANNUAL 2019

CONTENTS

 10

 16

 28

 32

 60

 68

52

HELLO! · 6

ALL ABOUT SPARKS · 8

THE BUILDER'S INVENTORY · 10

MARKETPLACE · 14

EMERGENCY BASE SURVIVAL CHALLENGE · · · · · · · · · · · · · · 18

BLOCK MUSEUM BUILD CHALLENGE · 22

MOJANG'S BUILD CHALLENGES · 26

GARDEN MAZE CHALLENGE · 30

COMMUNITY BUILDS · 32

APARTMENT BLOCK BUILD CHALLENGE · · · · · · · · · · · · · · · · · 36

REALMS – JAVA EDITION · 40

MINING BOARD GAME · 44

BUILDING CRAFTS · 46

PROTECT THE VILLAGE SURVIVAL CHALLENGE · · · · · · · · · · · 48

STORY MODE SEASON TWO · 52

MINECON EARTH · 56

BLOCKWORKS TOP FIVE BUILDS · 60

TEST YOUR BLOCK KNOWLEDGE · 64

LEGO MINECRAFT · 66

GOODBYE · 70

HELLO!

Welcome to the Minecraft Annual 2019! What an incredible 12 months it's been!

Since last year's Annual hit shelves, Minecraft has continued to grow in all kinds of directions. It's bigger, better and more beautiful! The underwater biomes have blossomed to life with colourful corals and fishy friends. Village life has become more exciting and perhaps a little bit more dangerous, too. All that, and you can play the game on more platforms, in more ways, with more people than ever before.

And that's just all the stuff in the game. Our amazing community (that's you, reader – take a bow) is larger and livelier than ever! This year, YOU helped us decide what to put in the game. You amazed us with your imaginative builds, inventive minigames and crafty creations – and shared your brilliance with other players on the internet, on Marketplace and on Realms. Some of our Marketplace creators have been successful enough to quit their jobs and make Minecraft stuff full time!

In every way it's been a year of building. In fact, we decided 2018 should be called exactly that: the Year of Building!

We hope you had as much fun as we did, and enjoy this look back across the year. In these pages you'll find celebrations of the incredible things you achieved – your ambitious creations, your adventures and experiences – and we also found room to pack in tips, tricks and challenges, too!

Hopefully it'll keep you busy well into 2019!

Marsh Davies
Mojang

ALL ABOUT SPARKS

Hi! I'm Sparks. It's great to meet you! You might recognise me from the official Minecraft magazine – I'm the builder of the team, and since 2018 is officially Minecraft's Year of Building I'll be popping up quite a lot in this year's Annual. Yay!

HELLO FROM SPARKS

SCOUT

BEAR

MONTY

SPARKS

Oh, goodness, an entire spread to myself! I'm not going to cry, I'm really not. Sniff . . . Anyway, here are a few things you need to know about me: I'm an architect and a redstone expert. I love stuff! I love my friends! I love animals! And most of all, I love building! The only thing I don't love is the dark, and the terrifying monsters that live in the dark. That's why the thing I love most is building impenetrable fortresses surrounded by reassuring traps. I particularly love lava rooms – they're so colourful and burny!

My three close friends are Bear, Scout and Monty, and they'll be making special guest appearances throughout this Annual. Bear's a survival expert, Scout can take down any hostile mob that crosses her path, and Monty loves learning about the natural world. Keep an eye out for them – they're very friendly and keen to help!

HOW TO DRAW SPARKS

Fancy a little off-screen creative time? Follow these simple steps to draw a fun, comic-strip version of me, as seen in the official Minecraft Magazine!

1 Grab a pencil and draw a rough, very light outline of me. It should look something like this. Don't press down hard – you'll want to colour over these lines later.

2 Find some coloured pencils or pens and colour in my face, hair and goggles. You don't have to copy this exactly – it's up to you which colours you use.

3 Now colour in my body. Again, you can copy this picture or you can choose your own colours if you prefer. And that's it! I'm finished!

DRAW SPARKS HERE!

THE BUILDER'S INVENTORY

2018 has officially been declared Minecraft's Year of Building! So what better time to do some building of your own? Here's a rundown of the blocks that building enthusiasts like me find most useful when creating new masterpieces. I hope it's helpful!

BUILDING
WITH SPARKS

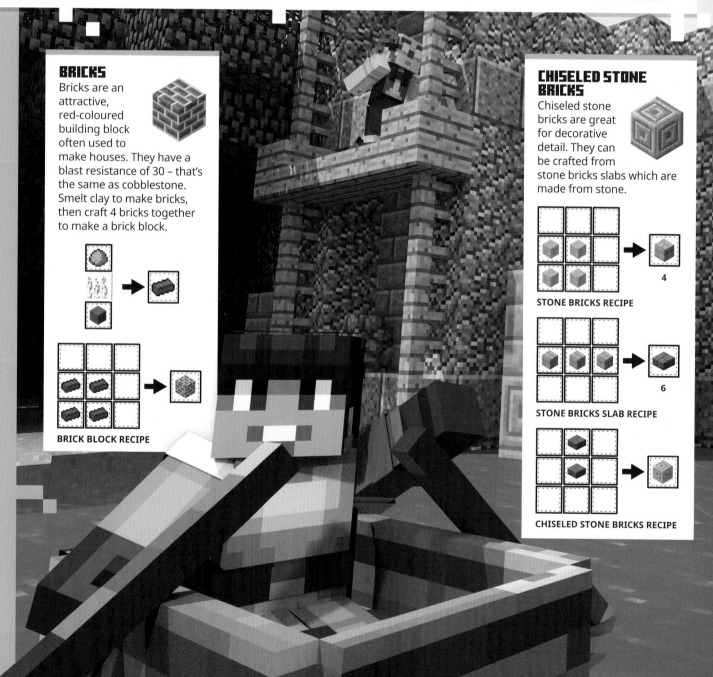

BRICKS

Bricks are an attractive, red-coloured building block often used to make houses. They have a blast resistance of 30 – that's the same as cobblestone. Smelt clay to make bricks, then craft 4 bricks together to make a brick block.

BRICK BLOCK RECIPE

CHISELED STONE BRICKS

Chiseled stone bricks are great for decorative detail. They can be crafted from stone bricks slabs which are made from stone.

4

STONE BRICKS RECIPE

6

STONE BRICKS SLAB RECIPE

CHISELED STONE BRICKS RECIPE

GLAZED TERRACOTTA

Glazed terracotta is great for decorative floors but its blast resistance is very low. It's produced by smelting stained terracotta which can be found in mesa biomes. Each colour produces a different variety.

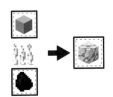

WHITE GLAZED TERRACOTTA RECIPE

CONCRETE

Concrete blocks come in 16 different colours, offering a rainbow of building blocks. Concrete is formed when concrete powder comes into contact with water. Concrete powder can be crafted from sand, gravel and your chosen dye.

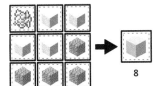

WHITE CONCRETE POWDER RECIPE

STAIRS

Stairs can be used to create a staggered tile effect for roofs. They come in all varieties of wood, cobblestone, bricks, sandstone, red sandstone, stone brick, Nether brick, quartz and purpur – you'll need 6 of each block to craft.

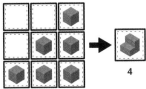

RED SANDSTONE STAIRS RECIPE

FENCES

Fences can be used to stop people falling from higher areas of your build such as balconies. They can be crafted from all 7 varieties of wood as well as Nether brick.

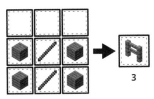

WOOD FENCE RECIPE

SLABS

Slabs are great for creating smaller build details like overhangs, windowsills and doorsteps as they're only half the size of a full block. They come in the same varieties as stairs.

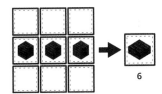

NETHER BRICK SLAB RECIPE

TRAPDOORS

Trapdoors can provide access to lower levels, and can be used to create rustic-looking windows that open and close. Wooden trapdoors can be found in 50% of igloos in ice plains biomes.

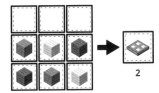

WOODEN TRAPDOOR RECIPE

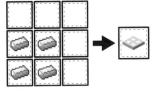

IRON TRAPDOOR RECIPE

GLASS

Glass is used to make windows to let light into your constructions. Smelt sand in a furnace to make glass blocks, which can be crafted into panes or dyed.

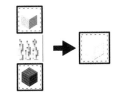

GLASS RECIPE

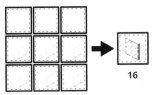

GLASS PANE RECIPE

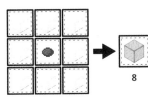

PURPLE STAINED GLASS RECIPE

DOORS

Doors are used to create switchable points of entry. They can be crafted from 6 varieties of wood, or iron. Several varieties of door can be found in naturally generated structures like NPC villages, strongholds and woodland mansions.

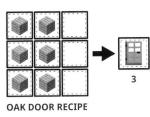

OAK DOOR RECIPE

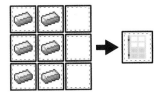

IRON DOOR RECIPE

THE BUILDER'S INVENTORY

NETHERRACK

Netherrack is ideal for fireplaces as it burns indefinitely once lit. It generates all over the Nether (it's the equivalent of dirt in the Overworld) and can be mined with a pickaxe.

SIGNS

Signs display text. They can also be used to conceal entrances. You can create items of furniture like sofas by placing signs on the side of stair blocks. They're crafted from wood planks and sticks.

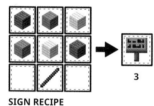

SIGN RECIPE

3

MOB HEADS

Mob heads make great features for bases. Dragon heads generate on End Ships on the Outer Islands. A wither skeleton may drop its skull when killed by a player or a tamed wolf. Skeletons, wither skeletons, zombies and creepers may drop their heads if killed by a charged creeper's explosion.

NETHER BRICK

Nether brick has a high blast resistance so it's a good choice for building bases. Nether fortresses are made from Nether brick and you can craft it from Nether bricks (Nether bricks are created by smelting netherrack in a furnace). You can also craft a red variant of Nether brick from Nether wart and Nether bricks.

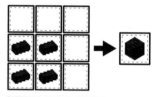

NETHER BRICK RECIPE

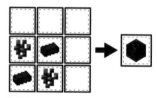

RED NETHER BRICK RECIPE

COBWEBS

Cobwebs are perfect for creating trails of smoke for chimneys. They can also be used in traps as they slow the movement of mobs and other players. They can be found in abandoned mineshafts, stronghold libraries, igloo basements and woodland mansions and will need to be mined with shears.

GLOWSTONE

Glowstone is an attractive light source often used for lanterns and chandeliers. When mined in the Nether, glowstone blocks drop glowstone dust, which can be crafted back into glowstone blocks.

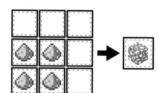

GLOWSTONE RECIPE

PUMPKINS

Pumpkins are an excellent addition to a spooky build. They can be found naturally growing on grass blocks across the Overworld. Craft a pumpkin with a torch to make a jack o'lantern which provides a spooky light source.

END STONE

End stone can only be found in the End. It has a blast resistance of 45 which is higher than other varieties of stone. This makes it a great block from which to build a sturdy base.

MAGMA BLOCKS

Magma blocks are ideal for building traps as they'll do damage to invaders even when hidden under a layer of snow, carpet, a redstone repeater or a comparator. They can be found in the Nether or crafted from magma cream.

MAGMA BLOCK RECIPE

SOUL SAND

Soul sand slows the movement of mobs or players, so it's another great block to use in traps. It generates all over the Nether, and under staircases in Nether fortresses.

BANNERS

Banners are customisable blocks that can be used to decorate your builds. A basic banner can be crafted from wool and a stick, and this can then be crafted with various patterns of dyes and other items to create many possible designs.

WHITE BANNER RECIPE

WHITE BANNER WITH BLACK CREEPER CHARGE RECIPE

PURPUR BLOCKS

Purpur blocks have a blast resistance of 30 so they're useful for building bases with a bit of colour. They can be crafted from popped chorus fruit, which is made from smelting chorus fruit in a furnace. Chorus fruit is obtained by breaking chorus plants, found on the outer islands of the End.

4

PURPUR BLOCK RECIPE

MARKETPLACE

EXPERT GUIDE WITH SPARKS

As I always say, the best thing about Minecraft is what the community makes with it. Discover just how creative the community is for yourself by visiting Marketplace — a store where you can browse and buy amazing community creations.

MASH-UP PACKS

 These packs contain everything you need to totally transform your world, from the landscape to your skin.

CHINESE MYTHOLOGY BY MINECRAFT

This mash-up pack offers a sprawling land of Eastern mystery, steeped in history and danger. There are ancient cities to explore, giant pandas and even dragons.

ADVENTURE TIME BY MINECRAFT

Dress up as your favourite characters from Adventure Time and explore the Land of Ooo with this colourful mash-up pack.

GREEK MYTHOLOGY BY MINECRAFT

This pack contains a custom texture pack and 39 character skins, from Zeus to Prometheus. Build a pantheon, trap the Minotaur in a maze or set sail to distant lands in search of adventure.

FALLOUT BY MINECRAFT

If you're a fan of the Fallout games then you're going to like this mash-up pack. There are 44 different skins to choose from, as well as a post-apocalyptic world complete with vaults.

WORLDS

Immerse yourself in these carefully crafted worlds full of danger and adventure.

LAPIS LAGOON BY IMAGIVERSE

This Japanese-themed water park offers endless hours of fun. But what really makes it special is the enormous Azure Dragon – it's an adventure slide and a quest to save the seasons all rolled into one epic build.

INFINITY DUNGEON EX BY JIGARBOV

Those who dare to enter this map will find parkour arenas, combat challenges, logic puzzles and more. You'll be hunting for items within the labyrinth to feed to the Infinity Core and, with any luck, escape from the dungeon in one piece.

DINOSAUR ISLAND BY PIXELHEADS

Ah, hubris! This tropical island has been overrun with dinosaurs after some unwise scientists lost control of their genetic experiments. There are four missions to complete, a modern laboratory and ancient ruins to explore.

THE CRATER BY BLOCKCEPTION

This survival spawn is set in a gigantic crater – presumably the result of some kind of meteor crash. Since the crash, some enterprising explorers have settled inside the crater and made it positively homely.

DESTRUCTOBOT 5000 BY NOXCREW

When the world is under attack from evil Robo-Aliens, you have only one choice: gear up and pilot the amazing DestructoBot 5000 mech suit. Your job is to hunt down the Robo-Alien bosses and save the world.

MONSTER BATTLE ARENA BY JIGARBOV

Ever wondered who would win a fight between an army of zombies and zombie pigmen, or spiders and witches? You're about to find out in this monster battle arena. Prepare mobs for battles then watch from the sidelines or join the fray.

MARKETPLACE

TEXTURE PACKS

Want to change the texture of the blocks, items and mobs in your world? Choose from an array of fun texture packs.

CITY TEXTURE
BY MINECRAFT

Become a Minecraft architect and shape the world around you.

FANTASY TEXTURE
BY MINECRAFT

This texture pack will transport you to a time when knights were heroes.

SKIN PACKS

Pick up one of these skin packs if you're looking to reinvent yourself before you head off on your next adventure.

VILLAINS
BY MINECRAFT

Feeling nefarious? With everything from a Dungeon Spectre to a Cake Maniac, this is the skin pack for you.

TOWN FOLK
BY MINECRAFT

It takes all sorts to make a town – whether you fancy yourself as a mime, a town crier, a thief or a witch, this texture pack has it all.

EMERGENCY BASE SURVIVAL CHALLENGE

Even an experienced survivor can find themselves in need of an emergency base. But a true survivor knows how to turn various naturally generated structures into safe places. Here are my recommendations for when you're really in a jam.

SURVIVAL WITH BEAR

WITCH HUTS

Witch huts are found in swamp biomes. But before you go barging in you'll need to make sure the witch isn't inside or you'll be in even more danger than you already are. Light it up with torches, barricade the door with any blocks you have to hand, and you'll be safe for a little while.

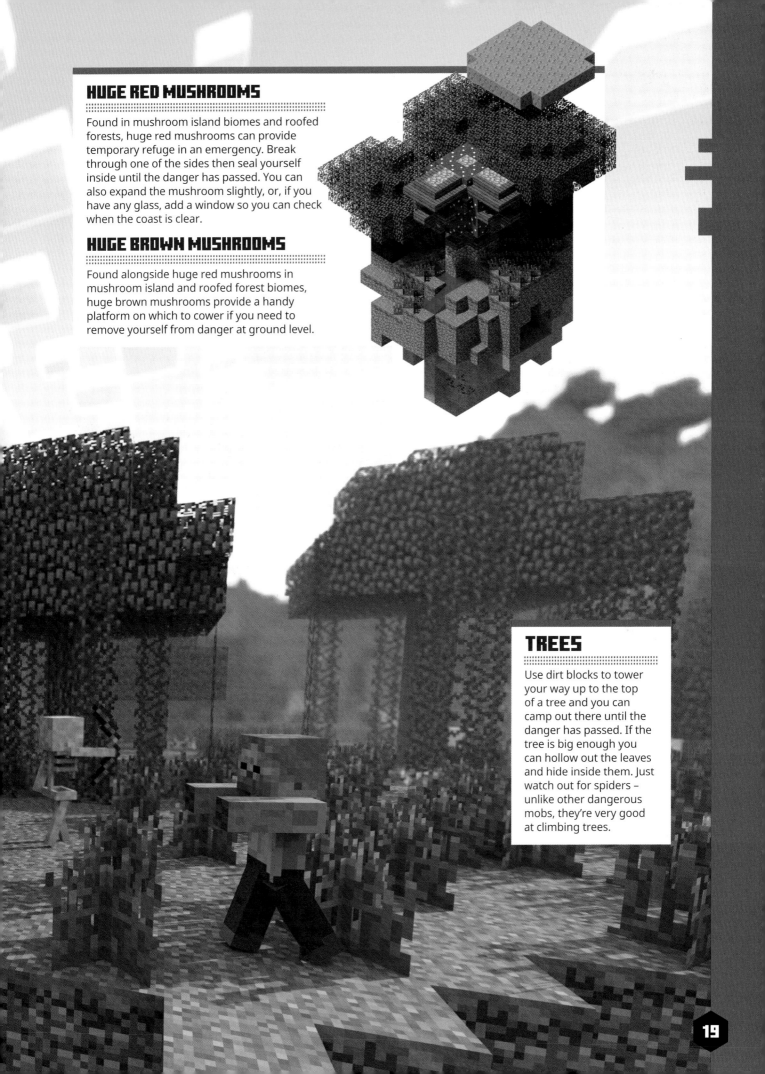

HUGE RED MUSHROOMS

Found in mushroom island biomes and roofed forests, huge red mushrooms can provide temporary refuge in an emergency. Break through one of the sides then seal yourself inside until the danger has passed. You can also expand the mushroom slightly, or, if you have any glass, add a window so you can check when the coast is clear.

HUGE BROWN MUSHROOMS

Found alongside huge red mushrooms in mushroom island and roofed forest biomes, huge brown mushrooms provide a handy platform on which to cower if you need to remove yourself from danger at ground level.

TREES

Use dirt blocks to tower your way up to the top of a tree and you can camp out there until the danger has passed. If the tree is big enough you can hollow out the leaves and hide inside them. Just watch out for spiders – unlike other dangerous mobs, they're very good at climbing trees.

19

EMERGENCY BASE SURVIVAL CHALLENGE

NPC VILLAGES

NPC villages offer several buildings in which you can take shelter. Churches offer the best protection, and a view of the surrounding area. Villages generate in desert, plains, savanna and taiga biomes. Just beware of zombies – they sometimes manage to break through wooden doors so you might want to upgrade to iron.

SMALL ISLANDS

If you get into trouble on the mainland and you can see a small island just off shore, swim across to it. Hostile mobs won't be able to follow you and it's much easier to defend yourself in a small space where mobs can't surround you. Just make sure you have some equipment to defend yourself if the need arises, and light up the island with torches to ensure no hostile mobs spawn.

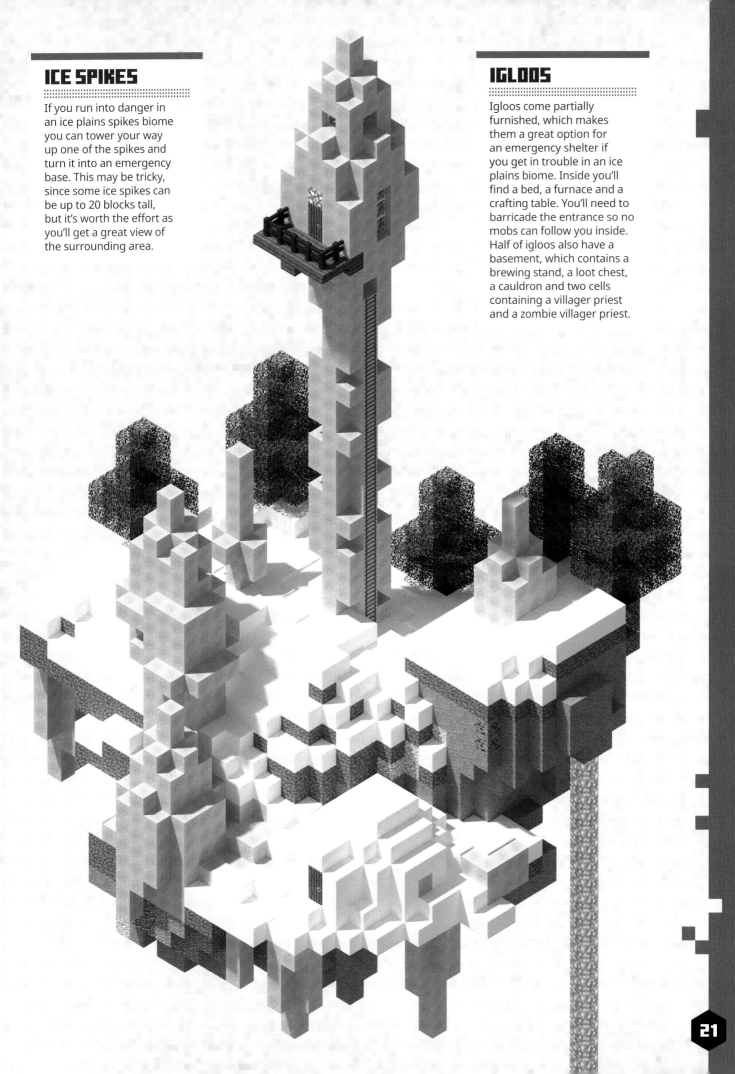

ICE SPIKES

If you run into danger in an ice plains spikes biome you can tower your way up one of the spikes and turn it into an emergency base. This may be tricky, since some ice spikes can be up to 20 blocks tall, but it's worth the effort as you'll get a great view of the surrounding area.

IGLOOS

Igloos come partially furnished, which makes them a great option for an emergency shelter if you get in trouble in an ice plains biome. Inside you'll find a bed, a furnace and a crafting table. You'll need to barricade the entrance so no mobs can follow you inside. Half of igloos also have a basement, which contains a brewing stand, a loot chest, a cauldron and two cells containing a villager priest and a zombie villager priest.

BLOCK MUSEUM BUILD CHALLENGE

PART 1

The most intrepid explorers pride themselves on discovering as many blocks as they can. I like to display each new block or item I find in my own private museum. Let me give you a tour, then you can build your very own block museum.

BUILDING WITH MONTY

1 COLOURS
The traditional features of this build don't lend themselves to bright, modern colours. The majority of the museum is built from polished blocks with muted colours, like various quartz blocks and polished granite.

2 PILLARS
Pillars are common on grand museums. They support the heaviest parts of the building and are usually built in one of three classic styles: Ionic, Doric or Corinthian.

3 DOME
Many grand museums have domes – semi-spherical structures that form part or all of the roof. They sit on cylindrical structures called rotundas.

4 ANVILS
Notice the use of anvils to outline the perimeter of the roof – they create an interesting area of detail and the dark colour is a dramatic contrast with the quartz.

6 BLOCKS
Each block you collect could be displayed on a plinth, or within an item frame mounted on a wall. You could also add signs to label each one.

5 WINDOWS
You don't want too many windows in a museum – you'll need all the wall space you can get to display your blocks.

BLOCK MUSEUM BUILD CHALLENGE

PART 2

BLOCK MUSEUM

🕒 2 HRS ❶❷❸ MEDIUM

If you'd like to copy my museum design exactly, this exploded build will help you get the details right. You can see the dimensions of each area of the build and how they fit together to form the museum. Don't be afraid to experiment and try your own thing, too!

BUILDING WITH MONTY

BUILD TIP

To begin with, build the basic walls and various floors of the museum. Exterior decoration and embellishments such as staircases, pillars and inset window features can be added on afterwards.

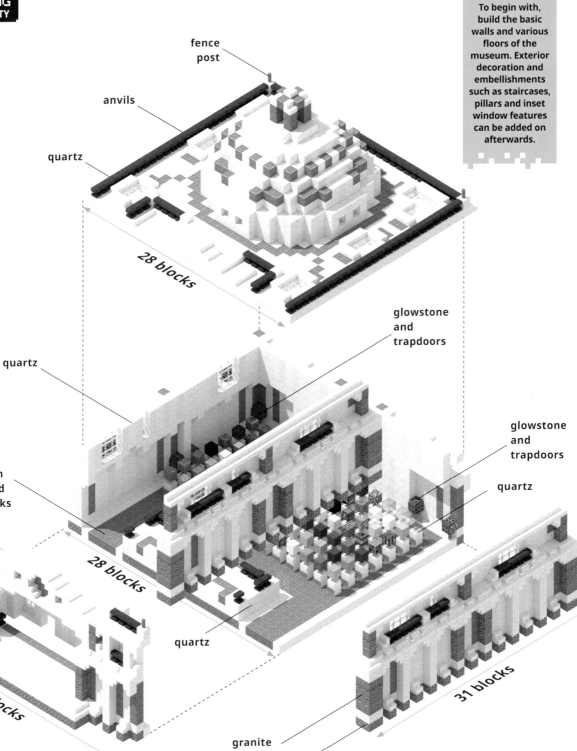

fence post

anvils

quartz

28 blocks

glowstone and trapdoors

quartz

glowstone and trapdoors

birch wood planks

quartz

28 blocks

quartz

28 blocks

31 blocks

granite

stone

MOJANG'S BUILD CHALLENGES

The Mojang team are a highly creative bunch who know how to have fun with their creations. So, who better to set some fun build challenges for everyone to try? See how many of these you can complete.

CHALLENGE TIME WITH SPARKS

DINO MODELS

You know who doesn't get a lot of love these days? The stegosaurus. It's been scientifically proven that they had the best fashion sense of all the dinosaurs, because they were rocking the sticky-uppy back plate things before they were cool. Every day I am saddened anew by their extinct status, so if you could be so kind as to build some stegosaurus buds to keep me company in Minecraft, that would make me very happy.

EMILY RICHARDSON
WRITER

GARDEN

Nature has always fascinated me, even when living in a busy city, so my challenge for you is to make a garden with an area for each of the crops (sugar canes, potatoes, carrots, wheat, beetroots – mmm, I love beetroots). Each crop must have its own garden and paths should connect each area. Add your personal style to it and dare to create different layouts inspired by the real world. Detail is everything!

KARIM WALLDÉN
HEAD OF COMMUNITY RELATIONS

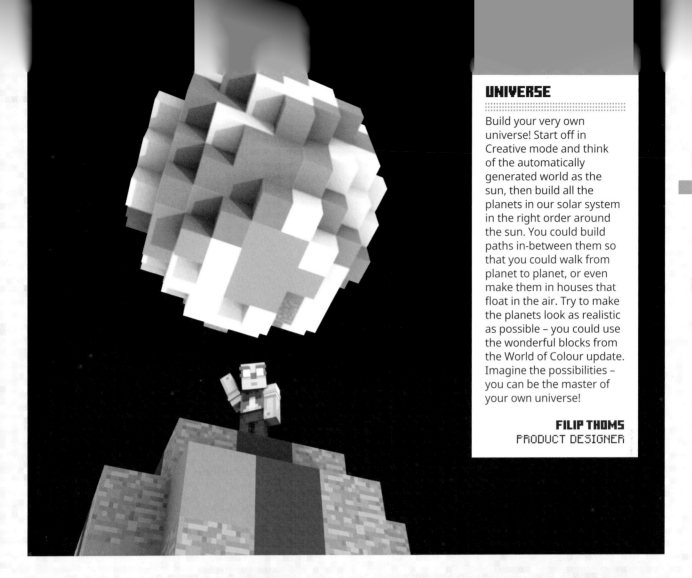

UNIVERSE

Build your very own universe! Start off in Creative mode and think of the automatically generated world as the sun, then build all the planets in our solar system in the right order around the sun. You could build paths in-between them so that you could walk from planet to planet, or even make them in houses that float in the air. Try to make the planets look as realistic as possible – you could use the wonderful blocks from the World of Colour update. Imagine the possibilities – you can be the master of your own universe!

FILIP THOMS
PRODUCT DESIGNER

JUNGLE RIVER RAFTING

Build a competitive jungle river rafting experience. Use twists and turns, obstacles such as small islands, and the occasional drop down a rapid or waterfall. It should be wide in places but narrow in others to create moments of competition with other players. Don't forget to design the shore and the background as well. If you're not experienced with world editing, consider starting with a default jungle biome and carving out an exciting river course. Add command blocks to determine the start and end of the race, and you're all set!

MARC WATSON
REALMS CONTENT CURATOR

MOJANG'S BUILD CHALLENGES

LLAMA CARAVAN

Build a llama farm and make a llama caravan. Make sure to give your llamas lots of hay and wheat and soon you should have enough llamas to make a caravan – you need at least 5 tame llamas and a lead. Remember that tame llamas carry carpets that they can wear that make them even cuter, and some carry chests that you can store your food or extra weapons in.

JENNIFER HAMMERVALD
PRODUCT DESIGNER

UNDERWATER GREENHOUSE

Building something in a surprising location or underwater is always cooler. So, your next challenge, should you accept it, is to build a glass greenhouse underwater, then light it up with some torches and get some sugar canes growing (if you want to earn 1337 points, do this without touching water!). I'd suggest you use this seed: -473705166 5092249714. If you do, I'd like you to tweet me a picture and the amount of time it took you to complete it.

PATRICK GEUDER
DIRECTOR OF
BUSINESS
DEVELOPMENT

WIZARD TOWER

Every wizard needs an epic tower. Standing several storeys tall, high up on a craggy mountain peak or ruined and overgrown deep in an enchanted forest, the choice is yours. For this build challenge we want you to construct your very own wizard tower – a home fit for a true mage. Your build can go in all sorts of crazy directions but should still be recognisable as an enchanter's base of operations. Think about the wizard that inhabits your tower and let their characteristics influence the build. Does your mage practise dark magic and wicked witchcraft or is she a conjurer of illusions and a brewer of magical potions? Be inspired by your backstory and let it be visible in both your exterior and interiors.

MAX HERNGREN
LEVEL DESIGNER

FURRY FRIEND

I'm a bit of a crazy cat lady, and when I'm not spending time with my cats I like to daydream about my cats, draw pictures of my cats and even build models of my cats in Minecraft. I challenge you to do the same with your pets! What better way to pay tribute to your wonderful cat friend (or dog friend, but cats are definitely better than dogs) than to craft a giant, detailed build of them in your favourite game?

AMANDA STRÖM
PRODUCT DESIGNER

GARDEN MAZE CHALLENGE

Nature-lovers like myself take great pride in sculpting the natural world. This maze has been in my family for centuries. Many people have tried to make it through to the end, and many have failed. Care to give it a try?

CHALLENGE
TIME
WITH MONTY

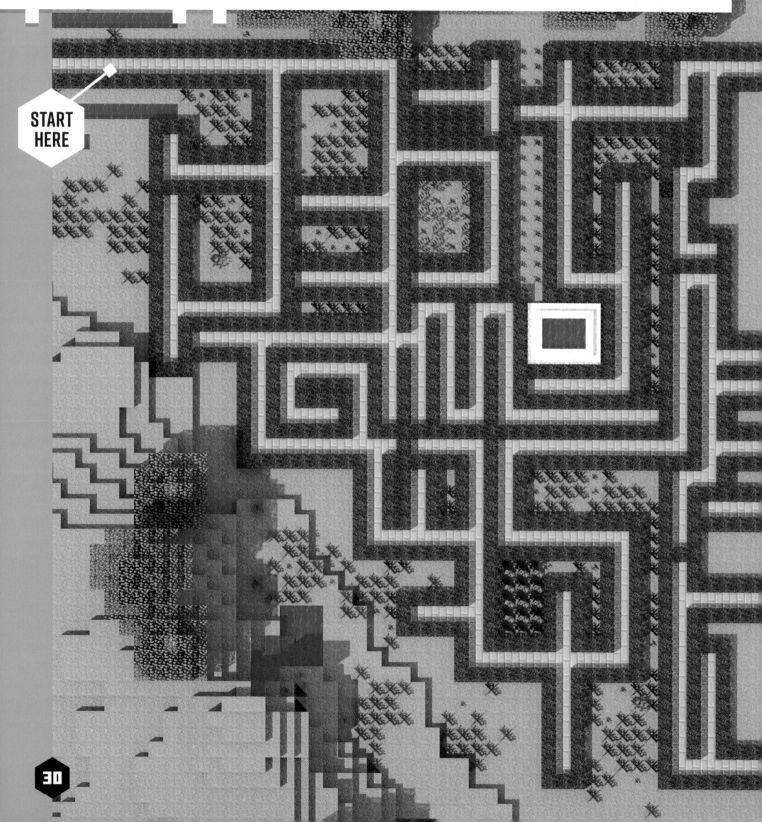

START
HERE

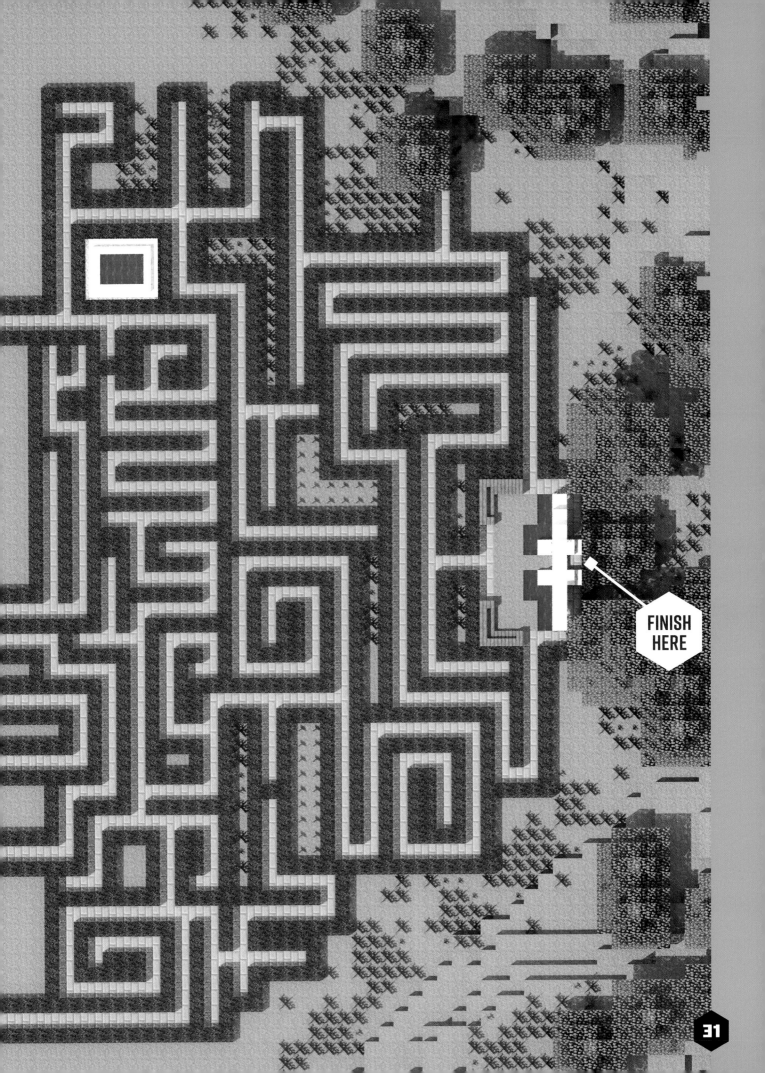

FINISH
HERE

COMMUNITY BUILDS

The Minecraft community is constantly producing an imaginative selection of builds for the rest of the community to marvel at. Head over to the official Minecraft website and you'll find an entire section dedicated to these builds. Here are some of my favourites to inspire you to create something epic of your own.

EXPERT GUIDE WITH SPARKS

GARRY THE GENTLESNAIL
BY ELI

This is Garry the Gentlesnail – he's a sharp dresser and he likes vegan food. In place of a shell he has a sprawling collection of builds – there's even a windmill. Everything has a purpose – inside the builds you'll find a complete working base including a living room, kitchen, bedroom with en-suite bathroom and an elevator.

Render by Rebelite

HUB GALAXIE
BY THE PERFECTION

This mini-galaxy is in a world of its own. It's a recreation of our very own galaxy, complete with planets, stars, comets and asteroids. Earth sits right at the centre, in the middle of the spawn point. The builder, The Perfection, created a wall of pixel-art stars to give the impression that the map was infinite.

MOUNTAIN OF MADNESS
BY JOSHUA

Fancy a winter holiday, Minecraft-style? Check out Mountain of Madness by Joshua – it's full of minigames, hotels and restaurants to explore, as well as working lifts to help you navigate the ski slopes. Minecraft doesn't have skis, but Joshua has provided an assortment of special footwear that will make you move faster and more powerfully down the slopes.

SAPPHIRE OCEAN
BY SQUITY

This underwater city is a tribute to ancient Greek architecture – it's a collection of ornate towers, temples and colosseums. And these impressive builds are surrounded by various sea creatures and plants to make visitors feel as if they're really in the ocean. There's even a giant orca whale and a Poseidon statue.

33

COMMUNITY BUILDS

MAN AGAINST NATURE
BY SAMANGA BUILD TEAM

This epic build depicts a battle between a giant stone golem and a group of lethal, man-made machines. It was inspired by the movie *Avatar* (take a look at the vehicles) and it took just two weeks to build.

WEDDING OF THE RAILS
BY THE WALSCHAERTS BUILD TEAM

This historical build is a recreation of The Golden Spike Ceremony that celebrated the completion of America's first transcontinental railroad back in 1869. The lead builder, Nathan_Oneday, wanted to go as big as possible with the scale to make sure he got the details right on the train – the people in the crowd are around 40-50 blocks tall.

WONDERLAND'S SANCTUARY
BY DENNISBUILDS

This is an island for people who have fled their homes and want to rebuild civilisation. Dennisbuilds likes working on fantasy builds because there are no rules. His island is a mish-mash of different architectural styles, and he's added several dragons swooping over the builds.

CATALNE
BY AEQUOTIS

This build is all about the detail of a quiet, rural life back in Medieval times. Set in a huge forest, it's easy to get lost as you explore. There are little villages, farms and streams dotted around, just waiting to be discovered. And don't forget to explore inside the buildings, too – the builder has hidden details in the most unexpected places.

APARTMENT BLOCK BUILD CHALLENGE

PART 1

Ooh, I just love visiting cities! So many epic buildings to look at! I've always fancied living in one of those modern apartment blocks. I spotted this one on my travels and I just can't wait to rebuild it! Why don't you have a go, too?

BUILDING WITH SPARKS

1 SPACE
Space is limited in cities, so many people live in apartment blocks that extend upwards into the sky.

2 GARDENS
Apartment blocks often have small, communal gardens where residents can enjoy a little bit of nature, even in the middle of a great city.

3 COLOURS
Modern architecture is known for its simplicity, its clean lines and its bold colours. The majority of this apartment block is grey and white, but the yellow blocks give it a little pop of colour.

4 BALCONIES
Balconies provide apartment block residents with a private, open-air space to enjoy. Stained glass panes are used to prevent residents from falling over the edge, and they match the grey walls of the main building.

5 LEVELS
The levels within an apartment block don't have to be identical – some levels can contain two or three apartments, whilst others may be dedicated to a single penthouse apartment.

APARTMENT BLOCK BUILD CHALLENGE

PART 2

APARTMENT BLOCK

⏱ **2 HRS** ❶❷❸ ✦ **MEDIUM**

Want to create an exact copy of the apartment block? Need a little help to get the details right? This exploded diagram shows you how to construct each part of the apartment block, including the apartment interiors.

BUILDING WITH SPARKS

BUILD TIP

Start with the frame of the apartment block, then the structural features like the stairwell. Creating rooms is much easier when there's a framework in place.

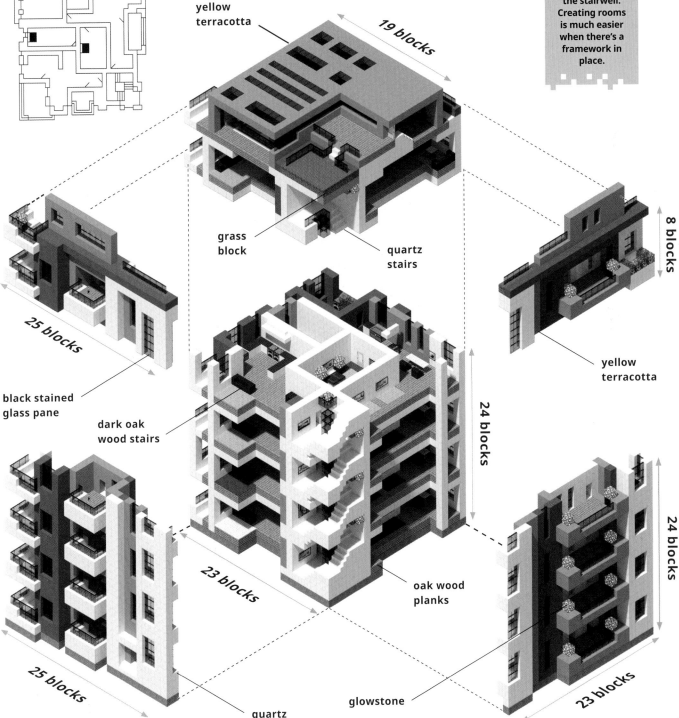

yellow terracotta

19 blocks

8 blocks

grass block

quartz stairs

yellow terracotta

25 blocks

black stained glass pane

dark oak wood stairs

24 blocks

24 blocks

23 blocks

oak wood planks

25 blocks

glowstone

23 blocks

quartz

REALMS – JAVA EDITION

The Java edition of Realms features some incredible maps, minigames and experiences, all made by the Minecraft community. And it's constantly being updated with exciting new content! Let's take a look at some of the highlights from the past year.

EXPERT GUIDE WITH SPARKS

> Since Minecraft's release, creation tools have exploded in number. Previously, innovative players made fantastic creations such as rollercoasters, replicas of spaceships, or working calculators. Now, there's no limit to the types of content that you can make. The magic of custom creations is not merely enabled by the game's code, but in the unexpected ways that players expand upon the game's features. We're continually delighted by what you do with Minecraft.

MARC WATSON
REALMS CONTENT CURATOR

MAGMA RUNNER
BY ROGUE_BARON

The goal of this game is to run as fast as you can to the bottom of the course before the magma catches up with you. Along the way you'll be rewarded with bonuses like TNT so you can blow up the floor, or cobwebs so you can slow your competitors. Choose from three difficulty settings, depending on how confident you're feeling.

QMAGNET'S TEST MAP
BY QMAGNET

This map was originally designed to test pretty much everything in Minecraft. It's basically a giant museum containing everything from a block display and an art gallery to a mob display room and a music and sound effect room. There's also a testing area where you can experiment with mobs and effects.

PENTABLOCK
BY INCARCERON, JBIP, DRAGONMASTER95

In this board game you're competing against another player to be the first to line up five pieces. And there's a literal twist – after placing each piece, you rotate one of the quadrants with the aim of foiling your opponent's plan or performing a winning move. You'll need to think carefully.

DIAMOND DEFENDER 2
BY XISUMA, POLLIEBOY AND VILDER50

In this explosive minigame you must protect diamonds from the creepers. You'll be subjected to 10 waves of increasingly-deadly creeper attacks, and you'll have to knock them into the Void before you can collect the diamonds. Choose from four difficulty levels and play on your own or team up with your friends.

CANTARA
BY JUSTTHATHAT AND INFIXES

This is a two-player board game where the number of spaces that you can move is determined by the colour of the space that you're standing on. Each player is given five major pieces and five minor pieces, and the winner is the first person to capture all of their opponent's major pieces.

REALMS – JAVA EDITION

NINJA DEFENSE
BY ROGUE_BARON

In this minigame you'll have to defend yourself against waves of ill-intentioned illagers. You'll need patience, dedication and precision if you want to succeed – the illagers will attack you from all sides, and your job, as a master of villager martial arts, is to defeat them before they reach you. It's game over if they get close enough to touch you.

METEOR MINERS
BY LIKEABAUS, 123MAARTEN123 AND YZEROGAME

The aim of this game is to build bridges across to asteroids made from ore blocks and mine the asteroids for resources and points. But you'll be fighting against the opposing team to get your hands on these materials and upgrade your equipment. You can shoot your opponents with lasers or spleef them into the Void.

BIOME RUN
BY SUPERSETTE

You'll have a mere four hearts of health as you navigate this parkour puzzle track whilst racing your opponents. If you take too much damage you'll respawn back at the beginning, giving your opponents the chance to win. You'll need to run the map several times to get the hang of it, so keep trying.

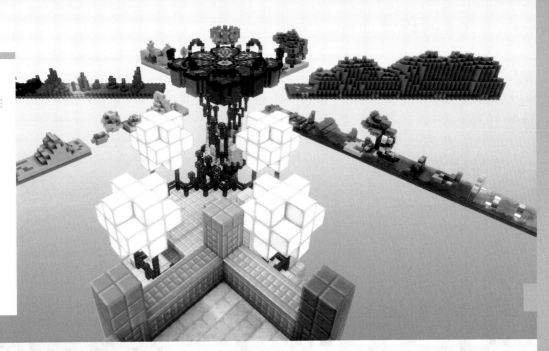

LEVITATE
BY 0SIRAWESOME

In most situations, being hit by a shulker projectile is an undesirable event. But in this minigame you want the projectiles to hit you so that you can levitate up to the slime block at the top of the arena. There are three unique arenas to try and various elements of the game that can be customised for endless rounds of fun.

COLOR CONTROL
BY SYBILLIAN

Color Control is a competitive, team-based minigame. The aim is to take over the cubes by mining them until they change to your team's colour. Then you'll need to defend them from the other team's players. You'll get points for each cube that your team controls and you'll also earn bonus materials as you go.

MINING BOARD GAME

For your next epic build you're planning a palace made from valuable ores. That means it's time for a dangerous mining expedition to the bottom of the world to collect materials. Find a friend to play with and race to complete your mining expedition.

CHALLENGE TIME WITH SCOUT

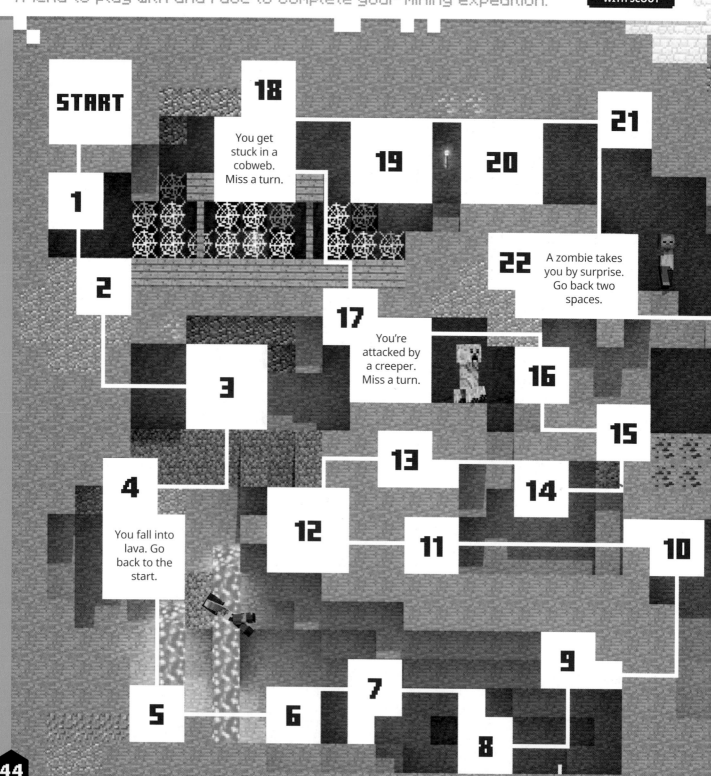

START

1

2

3

4
You fall into lava. Go back to the start.

5

6

7

8

9

10

11

12

13

14

15

16

17
You're attacked by a creeper. Miss a turn.

18
You get stuck in a cobweb. Miss a turn.

19

20

21

22
A zombie takes you by surprise. Go back two spaces.

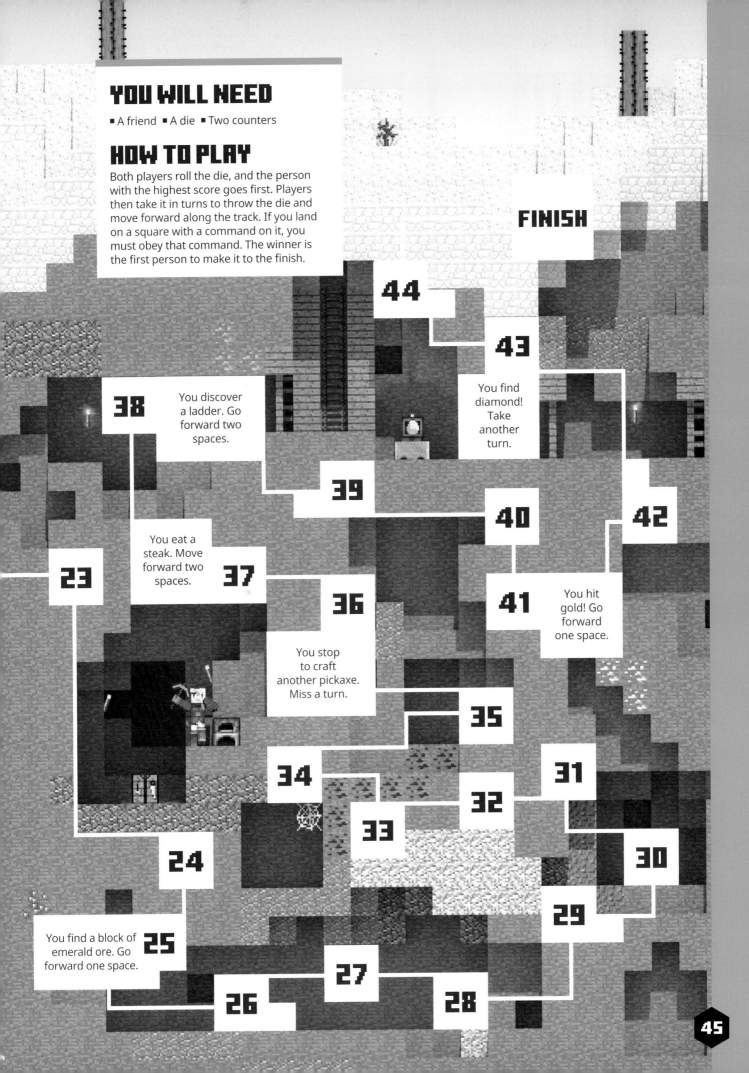

YOU WILL NEED

■ A friend ■ A die ■ Two counters

HOW TO PLAY

Both players roll the die, and the person with the highest score goes first. Players then take it in turns to throw the die and move forward along the track. If you land on a square with a command on it, you must obey that command. The winner is the first person to make it to the finish.

FINISH

44

43

You find diamond! Take another turn.

38 You discover a ladder. Go forward two spaces.

39

40

42

You eat a steak. Move forward two spaces. **37**

23

36

41 You hit gold! Go forward one space.

You stop to craft another pickaxe. Miss a turn.

35

34

31

32

33

30

24

29

You find a block of emerald ore. Go forward one space. **25**

27

26

28

BUILDING CRAFTS

Looking for some build-themed crafts to keep you entertained when you're not playing Minecraft? We've got some blocktastic ideas for you – create your own papercraft house and tree, and some awesome cake toppers for your next Minecraft party!

CHALLENGE TIME WITH SPARKS

YOU WILL NEED

- Thick coloured paper or thin card
- Tracing paper
- A ruler
- A pencil
- Scissors
- A ballpoint pen
- Paint
- Strips of card, sponge or an eraser
- Glue stick or double-sided tape
- Straws or round lolly sticks
- Thick card (e.g. a cardboard box)
- Masking tape
- Cakes

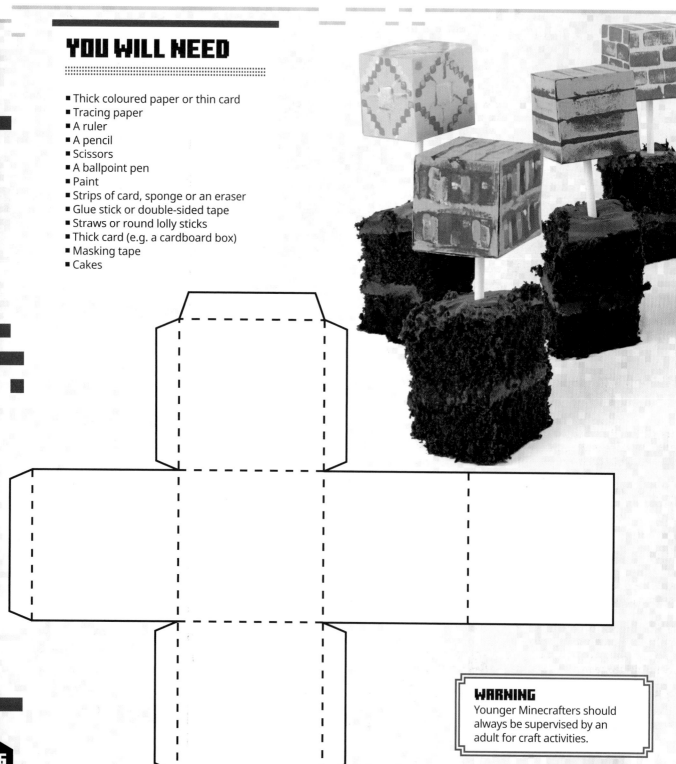

WARNING
Younger Minecrafters should always be supervised by an adult for craft activities.

HOW TO MAKE THE BLOCKS

1 Trace the block shape opposite onto some card, then carefully cut it out.

2 Draw round your shape on coloured paper or thin card, and cut it out. Score along the fold lines using a ballpoint pen.

TIP
If you're using dark card, use a light coloured pencil (e.g. white or yellow) to draw the outline.

3 Carefully fold along all the edges, then stick the block together using a glue stick or double-sided tape.

TIP
If you're using glue, wrap an elastic band around the block to hold it together until it has dried.

4 Print a pattern onto your block using a piece of sponge dipped in paint. You can copy the designs on this page or create your own. You could also use thick card or a piece of eraser. Leave the paint to dry. You could also use thick felt pens to add patterns onto the blocks.

5 To make a door, cut a rectangle from thick card and make it 2 blocks high. Cover the edges with masking tape, then paint.

6 Now you can use your blocks to construct your very own house and a tree. For the cake toppers, simply push cake pop sticks, lolly sticks or straws into the blocks, then use them to decorate your cakes.

PROTECT THE VILLAGE SURVIVAL CHALLENGE

There's nothing I dislike more than watching an angry horde of zombies attack a group of helpless villagers when darkness descends. Here's how to stop innocent villagers from being turned into nasty zombies intent on your destruction.

SURVIVAL
WITH SCOUT

1 LIGHT
Light up as much of the village as possible to prevent hostile mobs spawning in the dark areas. Build glowstone lanterns in strategic places throughout the village or add torches if space is limited. Remember to light up the insides of the buildings, too, to prevent mobs from spawning inside them.

2 DOORS
Zombies can only break doors if they're standing directly in front of them and your difficulty is set to hard. If you remove the block in front of the door so that the ground is a block lower than the door, or raise the door so it's a block higher than the ground, zombies won't be able to break in but villagers and players will still be able to jump inside.

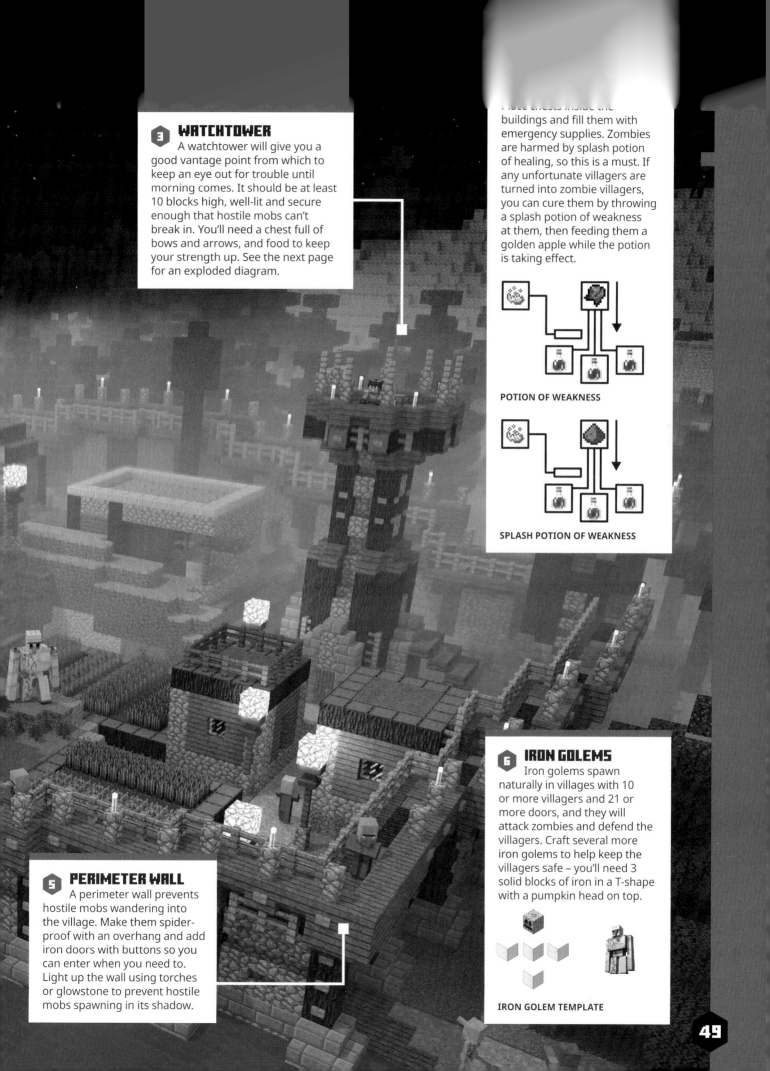

3 WATCHTOWER

A watchtower will give you a good vantage point from which to keep an eye out for trouble until morning comes. It should be at least 10 blocks high, well-lit and secure enough that hostile mobs can't break in. You'll need a chest full of bows and arrows, and food to keep your strength up. See the next page for an exploded diagram.

...ate chests inside the buildings and fill them with emergency supplies. Zombies are harmed by splash potion of healing, so this is a must. If any unfortunate villagers are turned into zombie villagers, you can cure them by throwing a splash potion of weakness at them, then feeding them a golden apple while the potion is taking effect.

POTION OF WEAKNESS

SPLASH POTION OF WEAKNESS

6 IRON GOLEMS

Iron golems spawn naturally in villages with 10 or more villagers and 21 or more doors, and they will attack zombies and defend the villagers. Craft several more iron golems to help keep the villagers safe – you'll need 3 solid blocks of iron in a T-shape with a pumpkin head on top.

IRON GOLEM TEMPLATE

5 PERIMETER WALL

A perimeter wall prevents hostile mobs wandering into the village. Make them spider-proof with an overhang and add iron doors with buttons so you can enter when you need to. Light up the wall using torches or glowstone to prevent hostile mobs spawning in its shadow.

PROTECT THE VILLAGE SURVIVAL CHALLENGE

PART 2

WATCHTOWER

🕐 0.5 HRS ④◇◇◇ EASY

SURVIVAL
WITH SCOUT

This exploded diagram shows you how best to construct a watchtower so you can keep an eye on the villagers and keep them safe.

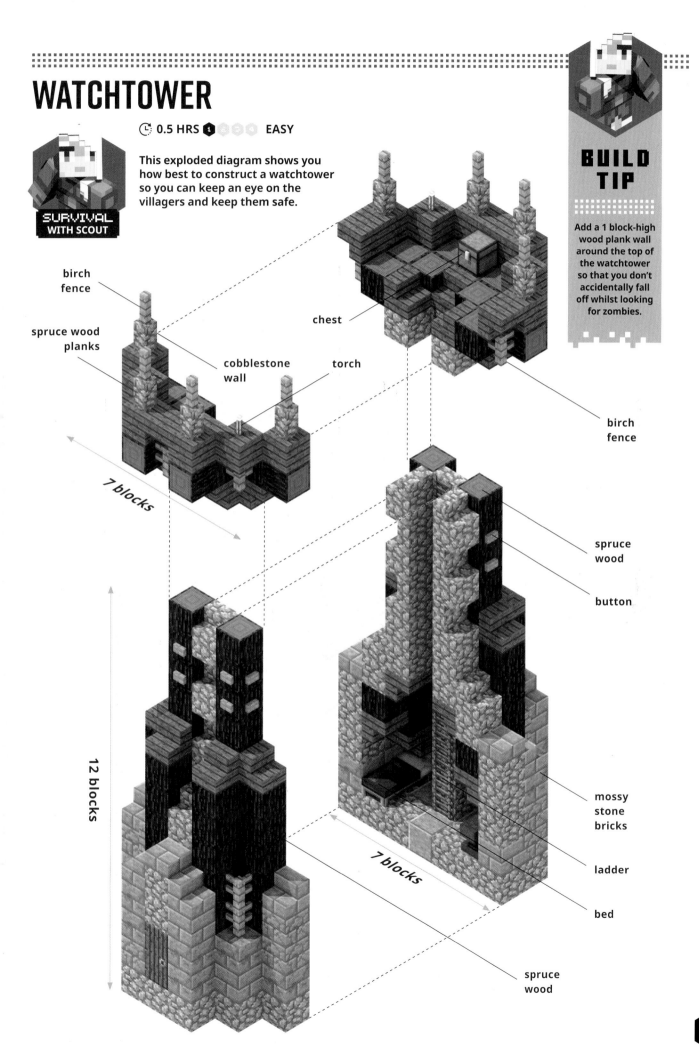

BUILD TIP

Add a 1 block-high wood plank wall around the top of the watchtower so that you don't accidentally fall off whilst looking for zombies.

birch fence

spruce wood planks

chest

cobblestone wall

torch

birch fence

7 blocks

spruce wood

button

12 blocks

7 blocks

mossy stone bricks

ladder

bed

spruce wood

STORY MODE SEASON TWO

SPOILER ALERT!
Contains spoilers for Season Two

EXPERT GUIDE WITH SPARKS

Season two of everyone's favourite spin-off game, Minecraft Story Mode, arrived in 2017. In this action-packed adventure you control the story through the main character, Jesse. And Jesse and the gang find themselves in mortal peril once again.

THE PLOT

Since Jesse and the gang managed to defeat the terrible Wither Storm and save the world they've become super famous. But it's made their lives more complicated – they have more responsibilities and less time for adventures, and for each other. They've begun to drift apart . . . But then Jesse's hand gets stuck in a cursed prismarine gauntlet that belongs to an ancient, underwater temple, and they find themselves plunged into a dangerous new adventure filled with tough choices . . .

JESSE

Jesse is Beacontown's leader, Hero-In-Residence and the character you control. After saving the world from the Witherstorm, Jesse has been taking it easy on the adventuring front, and has more responsibilities in Beacontown than ever before.

PETRA

Petra is Jesse's loyal best friend, and she's also a fearless warrior. Unlike the rest of the gang, she's on the lookout for her next big adventure and has absolutely no intention of settling down. Sometimes this lands her in trouble, but she knows that Jesse has her back.

RADAR

Radar is Jesse's excitable intern – he feels like the luckiest guy in the world. How he got the job is a bit of a mystery, but he really loves it, especially when Jesse leaves him in charge. He's very organised, although he's also a bit highly-strung, but he is always on hand to help Jesse.

STELLA

Stella is the leader of Champion City and claims to be Jesse's sworn rival, despite the fact that Jesse doesn't seem to have any idea who she is. She loves power and getting her own way and is prone to fits of jealousy. On a more positive note, she's a llama enthusiast, so she can't be all bad . . .

LLUNA

Lluna is a very special llama – she has the ability to sniff out treasure. What could be cuter than that? Stella is her owner, and together they live a life of luxury in Champion City. Lluna doesn't seem to like Stella very much, though, due to the way Stella treats her.

JACK

Jack has been called many names in his time. The Stab-Walker, He Who Slashes Like Thunder, The Velvet Tornado . . . All you really need to know is that he's a legendary treasure hunter who's been out of the game for some time. He currently runs a map shop with his best friend, Nurm.

NURM

Nurm is Jack's best friend and a cartographer villager with a passion for maps. He doesn't talk much, but he's very intelligent. He helps Jack to run the map shop and he secretly dreams of leaving Beacontown and travelling the world. Perhaps he'll get his chance soon . . .

STORY MODE SEASON TWO

THE LOCATIONS

Story Mode has its fair share of epic builds, and season two sees Jesse and the gang visiting some exciting new locations, as well as some old, familiar ones. Let's take a look at some of the best.

CHAMPION CITY

When you walk into Champion City you're greeted by a giant llama statue. Everything else in the city has been carefully colour-coordinated. Nothing is allowed in the city that doesn't look 'nice' or 'neat' – even the flowers are organised. It seems Stella has tricked the townsfolk into building it for her, exactly the way she wants it.

THE SEA TEMPLE

Jesse and the gang venture down to The Sea Temple in episode one, on a mission to find the mysterious Structure Block. Legend has it, it was built by a mysterious and all-powerful man known as The Admin. It's built from strange prismarine blocks that the gang don't recognise, and inside they find glowing obsidian blocks that turn out to be cages to hold prisoners. Eek!

THE ICE PALACE OF DESPAIR

In episode two, Jesse and the gang are challenged to retrieve a clock from The Admin's deadly Ice Palace of Despair. Much to their annoyance, the gang can't help but be impressed with The Admin's building skills when they arrive, and they're soon lured inside where they find an epic minecart system that makes them feel like they're at a theme park, and an archery arena. But it's not called the 'Palace of Despair' for nothing . . .

BEACONTOWN

Beacontown is Jesse's home and it's full of personality. Anyone can build anything in Beacontown, so it's a mish-mash of fun buildings designed by the townsfolk – there's a burger hot air balloon, a cow head, an upside-down house, a Reuben the Pig memorial and, of course, a giant beacon statue in the centre.

MINECON EARTH

In 2017 MINECON was replaced with MINECON Earth — a spectacular show that was broadcast all over the world, making it accessible to everyone. Let's take a look at the locations and some of the best bits from the show.

EXPERT
GUIDE
WITH SPARKS

SEATTLE

The live show was broadcast from the Museum of Pop Culture in Seattle. The show included a build battle, areas for people to play Minecraft on lots of different devices, a trivia contest and a chance to meet, question and get autographs from the developers who work on Minecraft.

LONDON

Hypixel ran an intense Skywars tournament at the Copper Box Arena in London. The winner of the tournament got to take home an awesome trophy.

MINECON EARTH

TEL AVIV

4DV held an official viewing party in Israel.

GUANGZHOU

Another official viewing party was hosted in China by NetEase.

JOHANNESBURG

Floating Tree hosted an official viewing party in South Africa.

MINECON EARTH

THE HOSTS

This year Lydia co-hosted MINECON Earth with Will Arnett. They even performed a song and dance routine to round out the show.

COSPLAY COMPETITION

The winners of this year's costume competition really thought outside the box. Father and son Chad and Noah dressed up as Jesse and the Wither Storm from season one of Story Mode.

NEW MOB

For the first time ever, the Minecraft community got to choose the next mob that would be added to the game as part of the Update Aquatic. There were four options and after a very close vote, mob B – the monster of the night skies – was declared the winner.

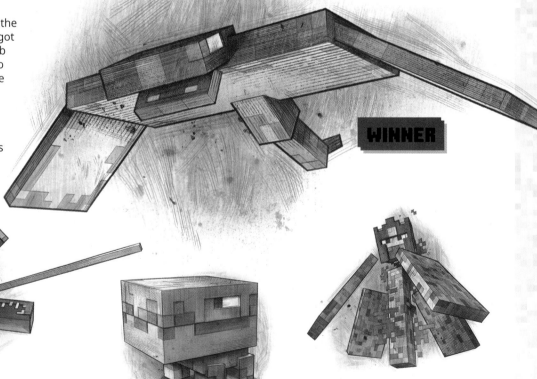

WINNER

ADVENTURE TIME MINECRAFT SPECIAL EPISODE

Minecrafters were treated to a first look at an all-new, full-length Adventure Time Minecraft special episode to be released in 2018.

THE UPDATE AQUATIC

Will interviewed Jeb about the Update Aquatic which was still in development at the time. Minecrafters were particularly excited by the addition of dolphins and the new trident weapon.

BLOCKWORKS TOP FIVE BUILDS

If you like building in Minecraft you've probably heard of Blockworks. They create all sorts of content for Minecrafters to enjoy, from adventure maps to learning environments. Here's what they have to say about their top five builds.

EXPERT GUIDE WITH SPARKS

5

CLIMATE HOPE CITY

We were asked by the *Guardian* newspaper to build a modern version of urban living in a clean and sustainable city in Minecraft. We needed to use existing green technologies and prototypes to create a positive image for sustainable living, which also seemed achievable and not too far off reality. The build is part of the *Guardian's* 'Keep It In the Ground' campaign. The city itself has a very organic layout, following curves and spirals. The main path of the map spirals towards the centre – a structure based on the dome of London's St Paul's Cathedral, which we have converted into a biodome.

TOMORROWLAND

Tomorrowland is a Utopian vision of a beautiful, futuristic city – built and lived in by the world's greatest minds. A place where anything is possible, it's an urban dreamworld of epic proportions. Built in partnership with Disney to celebrate the release of the blockbuster film, Tomorrowland, this was one of our first projects that used curved geometries to such an extent. Although curves are tricky to build, it was worth the effort to make this city look as futuristic as possible.

BLOCKWORKS INC.

This is the headquarters of the Blockworks building team. From this vast industrial complex we produce builds of all styles, themes and sizes and all of our building processes are presented for everyone to see. This whopping 100 million-block build was the winning entry to the Planet Minecraft 'Industrial Revolution' competition. Our concept of a 'build factory' is a figurative representation of the work and process of the team in the form of a Minecraft build.

FIRE 1666

To mark the 350th anniversary of the devastating Great Fire of London, we worked with the Museum of London to create three maps to educate a young audience about one of London's most infamous historical events. For the first map we rebuilt the entire area destroyed by the fire, including landmarks such as St Paul's Cathedral. We used maps and drawings in the Museum's collection to recreate seventeenth century London as accurately as possible, and we'd like to think we got pretty close!

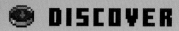
BLOCKWORKS
TOP FIVE BUILDS

DEEP SEA

From the depths of the ocean, from the fathomless world of infinite mystery and unearthly beauty which man has yet to discover, in first place is Deep Sea. This 32 million-block underwater laboratory has a plethora of facilities and technologies to aid in the study of the alien creatures the deep sea is host to. The concept behind this project was exploring the parallels of deep space and deep sea. Although space is considered mankind's final frontier, even today much of the deep ocean is a mystery and home to creatures just as alien as those we might imagine on other planets. The human element of this build is the large structural complex – an underwater laboratory which studies these underwater mysteries.

TEST YOUR BLOCK KNOWLEDGE

Fancy yourself something of a build expert, do you? Well, there's no better way to find out how much you know than through a quiz! I put this one together especially for you. See how many of these questions you can answer correctly. No cheating!

CHALLENGE TIME WITH MONTY

1 One side of this block looks a bit like a smiley face. Which block is it?

Dropper ✓

2 Which of the following blocks can endermen NOT pick up and move? Circle the correct answer.

a) TNT
b) Cactus
c) Red mushroom
d) Stone (circled) ✓

3 This block is a light source and can be retrieved from ocean monuments in deep ocean biomes. Write its name here.

sea lantern ✓

4 This block is a variant of stone with a pink hue.

✓ Granite ✓

5 Which tool will mine clay the quickest? Circle the correct answer.

a) Pickaxe
b) Shovel (circled) ✓
c) Hands
d) Hoe

6 Which two ingredients do you need to craft a bookshelf?

~~oak~~ planks and books ✓

7 Which of these blocks has the lowest blast resistance? Tick the correct answer.

 Obsidian ☐ Nether brick

☐ Diamond ☐ Iron door

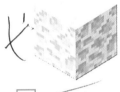 

☑ End stone ☐ Bricks

8 This is the smallest block in Minecraft.

buttons ✓

9 If you walk on this block your movement will be slowed.

soul sand

10 This block is bouncy and can be used to make trampolines.

slime block

11 Which block is this a recipe for?

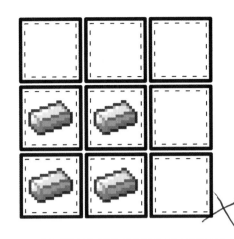

Iron Pressure Plate

12 Which of these blocks give out light? Tick as many as you think.

☐ Dragon head ☐ Brown mushroom

☑ Redstone ore ☐ Dragon egg

1/3

☐ Red mushroom ☐ Gold ore

Check your answers on page 70

DISCOVER

LEGO MINECRAFT

When the first LEGO Minecraft set was released in 2012 the Minecraft community rejoiced. Now they could enjoy their favourite game away from the screen, too! Let's find out which of the amazing LEGO sets are the Mojang team's favourites.

EXPERT
GUIDE
WITH SPARKS

THE ICE SPIKES
NUMBER OF PIECES: 454

I'm a big fan of the Ice Spikes LEGO set. For one thing, it's just a really striking and mysterious biome with all those tall blue spires! But there are also loads of neat details that help you tell cool stories about why you are there: lapis ore, an enchantment table and Steve's own enchanted pickaxe. You can fill in the dots yourself. The set is cleverly constructed out of modules that you can easily recombine in new ways without disassembling the entire thing. Plus, the snow golem actually fires snowballs! The very definition of cool.

MARSH DAVIES
HEAD OF CREATIVE WRITING

THE OCEAN MONUMENT

NUMBER OF PIECES: 1122

My favourite is the Ocean Monument because I loved designing that for the game, and it's amazing to see it as a LEGO set.

JENS BERGENSTEN
LEAD DEVELOPER

THE MOUNTAIN CAVE

NUMBER OF PIECES: 2863

My favourite set is the Mountain Cave. Nathan and I spent four hours putting together the huge build, and from a structural framework eventually came the mountain that our minifigures would call home. The best parts were the light-up redstone, the awesome, electrified creeper, and the minecart elevator. The elevator makes me want to connect it with the rails from other sets and just build rollercoasters!

MARC WATSON
REALMS CONTENT CURATOR

GO MINECRAFT

WARNING
Always check the age rating on a LEGO set. Younger Minecrafters should use LEGO sets with adult supervision.

THE ENDER DRAGON
NUMBER OF PIECES: 634

My favourite LEGO Minecraft set is the Ender Dragon set, because Ender dragon, and black bricks are always cool to build with.

PATRICK GEUDER
DIRECTOR OF BUSINESS DEVELOPMENT

My favourite LEGO set is the Ender Dragon. I have to confess that I have yet to reach the dragon in the actual game – I kind of suck at killing hostile mobs. Anyway, dragons are pretty cool (just as long as they can't kill you) and I really enjoyed building this with a friend's daughter.

ANNA KLINGBERG
BRAND ENFORCER

THE CRAFTING BOX

NUMBER OF PIECES: 518

My favourite LEGO Minecraft set is the Crafting Box because it comes with many different build ideas and it very much inspires me to build my own things.

DANIEL WUSTENHOFF
DEVELOPER

THE SNOW HIDEOUT

NUMBER OF PIECES: 327

I like the Snow Hideout set for two reasons, the first of which is SNOW. Snow is one of the greatest things that nature has to offer because it's a building material, but it's also fun. A bit like LEGO itself – although skiing through LEGO sounds like it would be pretty hard work. The second thing I love about this set is the SNOW GOLEMS. What's not to like about automated defence systems? They even come with a cheeky smile!

EMILY RICHARDSON
WRITER

GOODBYE

Gosh! What a way to send off 2018. Thanks for joining us on the journey!

As action-packed as this year has been, there's no time for us to kick back and relax: 2019 is Minecraft's anniversary year, and we're planning some pretty crazy stuff to make it extra special. With your help, we know it will be! So watch out for that! In the meantime, happy 'crafting.

Marsh Davies
Mojang

ANSWERS

30-31:

64-65:

1. Dropper
2. d) Stone
3. Sea lantern
4. Granite
5. b) Shovel
6. Wood planks and books
7. Iron door
8. Button
9. Soul sand
10. Slime
11. Iron trapdoor
12. Brown mushroom, redstone ore, dragon egg

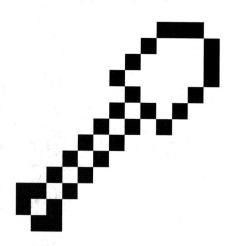